I0504959

Sales Surge Sequel:
Another 50 Secrets to Boost Your
Sales Success With Less Stress and
More Fun!

By Henry Oliver

Books by Henry Oliver

on Amazon and Audible

Sales Surge: 50 Secrets to Propel Your Sales Career With Less Stress and More Fun!

Sales Surge Sequel: Another 50 Secrets to Boost Your Sales Career With Less Stress and More Fun!

For the full list of awesome resources, authors and books we mention in this book, visit:

SaleSurgeBook.com

For you, the true sales professional, who is proud of the value you bring every day. With daily improvement, you can have the low-stress, exciting career you've always wanted. And as you succeed, you will improve the lives of countless customers, clients and colleagues. What a great opportunity!

Table of Contents

Introduction

Why do some sales professionals launch to seemingly instant success, while others languish for months, years or decades?
Why does it seem to come so naturally for some salespeople, while many continue to work - day in and day out - for small and fleeting results?
Why do some sales pros build a long-term career free of stress and full of prosperity, personal growth and fulfilling relationships?
Are there secrets that sales winners understand and put into action that others do not?

This book will continue pulling back the curtain on the real world of professional sales, so you can reach toward the success you've been dreaming of. As you learned in the first book, *Sales Surge: 50 Secrets to Boost Your Sales Success with Less Stress and More Fun!*, there are no guaranteed results, and this book won't be a magic wand to instantly transform your career from mediocre to off-the-charts awesome. But what it will do is help you improve and make you better than you are today.

In the pages that follow, you'll realize that you may already be incorporating many of these 50 secrets into your daily sales activities. Especially if you read the first book and put those tips into action! Perhaps many more of the "secrets" are techniques you can put into effect today to help you improve and grow. Because the truth is, they aren't secrets at all. These are proven success principles and tips that have been used and taught by successful sales professionals for centuries. In fact, we'll continue highlighting and linking to other thought leaders, books and resources that can help you continue your journey toward higher levels of sales success. This is the continuation of a journey that never ends.

You deserve a sales career that takes off and surges to higher levels.
You deserve a career with less stress and much more fun and enjoyment.
So let's continue!

The next 50 secrets...

51 Spend in proportion to the opportunity.

This relates to all available resources, including time and money. If the opportunity is extremely large, you can justify spending a lot of time and/or money in working on the deal. If the final result would be relatively small, regardless of your investment, then you'd be wise not to spend much of either your time or money. Even when working for a large sales organization, try to see yourself as owning your own business. Run your territory as your own, and make decisions you would make if it were your own money and time. Are your spending decisions justified by the final results of the sale? Are you spending $11 to make $10? Or are the efforts and expenditures - both time and money - going to produce a long-term, increasing return? These are dynamics to think about when considering what to spend in pursuit of an opportunity.

52 Be proud of what you do.

Sales professionals bring value. We improve the lives of our customers, and if we did not they would not trade their dollars for our products and services. Aren't most things we possess ultimately purchased from someone else? Do these purchases enhance our lives or detract from them? Of course, we gain satisfaction, joy and utilitarian value from each and every purchase we make - just as our customers do. I couldn't live without my iPhone or my favorite morning coffee mug! (slight exaggeration….and it's actually the *coffee* I couldn't do without.) Wake up every day ready, able and enthusiastic about improving the lives of your clients and customers. They are counting on you!

53 The home-office dilema.

"You are so lucky to work from home!"
"You have the life, laying around in your pajamas all day!"
"You must not work hard at all since you don't have to leave your house."
These are some of the many reactions you'll probably receive when working from a "home" office. But let's face it, these impressions are not only false, they fail to take into account the additional challenges of working out of a home office. Yes, working from a home office can be convenient, mainly because you can get right to work, anytime, without the time, effort and cost of a commute. The downside is that you often will find yourself getting right to work - during days, evenings, weekends or in the middle of the night! Work never leaves you when you work from home. And there is a strange phenomena where many people in your life - friends, family, neighbors - think that just because you are *home* you are not *working*. They think they can stop you to chat or take up your time, because you are HOME! These time-draining challenges must be managed in order

to succeed at working from a home office. Yes, the conveniences outweigh the downside, but the home office is a working environment that must be diligently managed and controlled to maximize your effectiveness.

54 All sales are not equal.

Some sales are one-and-done, with zero follow-up or support. Other transactions include many follow up visits to onboard, train and help execute the product or service. Other types of sales require constant refreshers, keeping your product or service top-of-mind for the customer. As professionals, we will usually reach our highest levels, in terms of happiness and financial rewards, when we align with the sales process and cycle that best fits our talents, abilities, experience and personality. For example, if you are a people-person who experiences a great deal of satisfaction with holding your customer's hand and providing excellent service, you would want to find a sales position that falls into this type of model. For you, the one-time transactional sale would not allow you to use your unique traits and best talents. Sure, you may succeed, however long-term sales success and happiness occurs when we most closely align ourselves with a sales process that fits our unique set of skills, interests and personality traits.

55 Know when to unplug.

When doing it right, sales should be a profession that permeates your life. You can just as easily talk about your product in a customer's office as you could on a weekend boating trip with your buddies. This is true of any career, by the way, in which a person has a true passion and deep connection with his or her work. But when your life is so intertwined with your sales career, we must all take deliberate, intentional time to back away and put our work aside. Do you find yourself checking sales reports on the weekend? Are you emailed customers while sitting in the stands at your child's sporting event? Sometimes it is not only wise to unplug - it is necessary. You must stay fresh and prevent burnout. We need to force ourselves to regularly put the computer, email, reports and work activities aside. We need to maintain the balance of our life, making sure we are devoting the necessary time and effort in all areas we find important in life - family, friends, health, recreation, etc. There is a reason we are told to rest on the Sabbath - because we need to refresh and rejuvenate, physically, mentally, emotionally and spiritually. Sales can be exhilarating, stressful and all-consuming, and we need regular intervals to unplug and put it aside, so we can maintain our highest levels for our work and personal life.

56 Sales should be fun!

Whether you sell high-end medical equipment in a hospital operating room or advertising space in the local periodical, you should have a regular feeling of enjoyment. Your product or service should improve your customer's life, otherwise why would they ever buy it. So if true, we need to enjoy the fact that we are bringing so much value! The great personal development leader, Jim Rohn, used to say, "Nothing happens until someone sells something." We are literally out there making things happen. We are getting the engine of commerce spinning, and improving the lives of our customers in the process. Additionally, humans are goal-driven beings, and we gain high levels of satisfaction by overcoming challenges and obstacles. We weren't meant to plod along with each day no more challenging or different than the last. Cats and dogs were made for that type of environment. Humans need to be challenged. Sometimes to fall short, but often to succeed, become better and achieve higher levels of success. Sales helps us satisfy these innate human needs, and when done right, this should be a fun profession!

57 Yes, you must close.

You must ask for the business if you want it. You earn the right to ask for the business by providing value, teaching and educating. You show how your product will truly help your customer. You build the relationship along whatever length buying cycle you work under, and then you ask for the commitment. If you don't ask for the commitment, it sends a subtle signal to the customer that you, yourself, aren't sold on the value you are proposing to deliver. If *you* can't even ask for the sale, it means you don't really believe it is in your customer's best interest. After all, if you believed this with all of your being, you couldn't help but close! It would be negligent to NOT close. So build the relationship, find out if your product is the right fit, and then ask for the sale.

58 Who are your mentors?

We all need experienced professionals who can share their experiences with us. We need people who have done what we want to do and have been where we want to go, so we can emulate their example and avoid their mistakes. Sound difficult to find these kinds of people? It isn't hard at all, because these mentors must be neither alive nor in your geographic area. A mentor might be Napoleon Hill, Zig Ziglar, a manager or a sales leader in your local market. We can, and must, learn from their wisdom and experiences - through books, podcasts, videos or personal encounters. Living in the technological age that we do, there is literally no excuse for having a steady supply of mentors, ready to lead us down the path of sales success.

*To learn more about the people and books we've highlighted, visit: **SaleSurgeBook.com**

59 Be proud of the value you bring.

Every human being is in sales, regardless of if we realize it. We are constantly selling…..to our spouses, our employers, our customers, our friends and ourselves. For some reason, however, our society has stigmatized the *profession* of selling. Nobody grows up and wants to become a *salesperson*, because that title is equated to the stereotypical used car salesman - pushy, sleazy and unethical. Provided you aren't accurately described by those adjectives, you can, and should, be proud of the value you bring as a professional salesperson. Politicians, leaders, entrepreneurs, dreamers, visionaries and teachers are all salespeople! They bring value and transmit that value, with enthusiasm, to their intended audience. Can you be proud of being a visionary? How about being a teacher? Of course you can! This is the same pride and enthusiasm you should emit regarding the profession of sales.

60 Sell today, invest long-term.

A sale today is built on a trust-filled relationship, which may lead to continuous and larger sales tomorrow. Providing exactly what you've promised, and more, will lead to future sales and referrals. This is one level of selling today and investing long-term. We also want to work smarter, not harder, by allowing our commissions to work for us. By following this formula, we can perform magic and turn today's sales into much larger sums tomorrow. And if you put your commissions to work, earning interest, they will continue to grow and multiple. For example, if I earn a commission of $100 for selling my product, I can easily pocket the Benjamin and spend it on something nice. But what if I put that $100 away and didn't touch it for 20 years? I still make only that one sale, but if it were earning just 10% interest for those two decades, it would grow to $732. So for the same sale, I earned either $100 or $732. Even when considering inflation, selling today and investing long-term can turn small commissions into large ones.

61 You can always learn something new.

There isn't a day that goes by where we can't pick up some new information to help us grow as a professional. It may be a helpful book, an article, a podcast or a conversation with a colleague or mentor. Each little pearl of knowledge is an arrow in your quiver. You never know when you can use that nugget to your advantage - to further a sale, delight a customer or aid a friend. Tiger Woods, considered by most to be the best golfer ever to play the game, has occasionally implemented this strategy to continue improving. At least a couple times in his career, and at the top of his game, he endeavored to revamp his golf swing. Why would the best golfer in the world want to *change* his swing? Because now he employs a consistently better swing, plus he has the older versions at his disposal should he ever see a need to use them. Even the best can reach for better. Every day is a learning day, and every true professional is continuously learning his craft.

62 Be the expert on your product.

Your customer will have questions, and you need to have the answers. For most questions, the answers must be ingrained, natural and memorized. For more complex, one-off questions, it is perfectly fine to acknowledge that you don't have the answer and follow up later. Customers know that we don't know everything and, as long as it is not a trend, they will extend grace when we need to get back to them. In fact, that follow-up will go a long way to distinguish yourself as someone who does what he says he will do. If we say we will get back to them with the answer, we need to get back to them with the answer. This builds trust. If they can trust you in the little things, they'll feel they can trust you with larger commitments.

63 Stand out and get noticed.

You will stand out when you show up every day with a mindset aimed at consistent excellence. Customers, prospects, managers and colleagues will notice. Your reputation will precede you when you consistently deliver more than what is expected, with a smile. Most sales professionals, and even a higher percentage of non-goal-based employees, strive to do the bare minimum. They want to do the minimum amount that will allow them to hold onto their jobs, while never peeking at what lies just beyond if only they'd give just a bit more effort. Put blunty, most people never even try to do anything more than the bare minimum requirement. The key to standing out, then, is to follow the biblical advice of "Going the extra mile." If someone asks you to walk a mile with them, walk two. If a customer asks you to spend ten minutes helping to train their team, spend 20 minutes. If a customer has some questions over the phone, stop by in person to assist them. When your manager says he has a project for the team, take the initiative and offer to help. Go the extra mile. You'll stand out for all the right reasons, and you can't help but succeed.

*To learn more about the people and books we've highlighted, visit: **SaleSurgeBook.com**

64 Kill with kindness.

Whenever possible, go above and beyond to delight your customers. When they are right, show your kindness. When they are wrong, show your kindness. When customers have choices, to buy or not to buy, and when they have competitive options, from which they can pick and choose, kindness will often carry the day. Just ask yourself....even when the customer is wrong, what do you have to gain by being unkind? Nothing! If there were unkind and NOT buying from you, you have nothing to lose, but everything to gain. Nine times out of ten they may never appreciate your efforts or buy from you. But that one out of ten will be a victory you earned only by being kind. Was that such a heavy lift?

65 Know when to walk away.

Some customers and some situations simply aren't worth it. They aren't worth the time, effort and drain on your resources. It may be a belligerent customer, or an unreasonable set of expectations. Is this someone who gets his jollies by tormenting vendors and partners? If so, your professionalism isn't deserved. Fire this customer and terminate the relationship. Sometimes you need to walk away and never return. Or perhaps the person is right but the timing is completely wrong. For example, you plan to have a very impactful conversation with a prospective customer, however when you arrive they are in the middle of an emergency situation. Rather than throwing your needs onto their plate at the moment, walk away. Be self-aware enough to realize that your visit will only cause more pain, rather than a solution at this moment. Walk away and come back another day.

66 Treat them all with respect.

This refers to the secretary, the janitor, the parking lot attendant and the intern. Everyone. Besides being the right way to treat people, you never know when this will put you in good standing. For example, have you ever called on a customer and initially had to deal with the secretary. Your goal is to get to the decision-maker, however the secretary is acting as a very effective gatekeeper. Only later do you realize this secretary is the spouse of the decision maker, and every interaction you've had has been filtered for the decision maker's review. How have you portrayed yourself and your company? Have you been respectful and made the secretary feel important? Have you valued the secretary's time? Treating everyone with respect puts you in the best position possible to have an impact with this new customer. Plus, it's just the right thing to do.

67 Fail as often as possible.

If you aren't failing, you aren't trying. And if you aren't trying, you'll never win - not a deal, not a sale, not a President's Club award, not a promotion and certainly not long term, stable success. The basic rules of sales still apply - it is a numbers game, and the more NO's you get, you'll get closer to a YES. The better your product, your skills, your talent and your drive, the better that ratio will be. John Maxwell lays it out perfectly in his fantastic book, Failing Forward. Maxwell urges us to "make failure our friend," propelling us toward higher success. So expect to fail as you expect to win, because only through failing can we reach toward, and achieve, higher levels of achievement.

*To learn more about the people and books we've highlighted, visit: **SaleSurgeBook.com**

68 Prove that customers love what you have to offer.

Social proof is one of the most effective ways to connect with a customer - *showing* how others in similar situations have gained great value from what you offer. Doctor Robert Cialdini, in his classic book, Influence, details the massive power and effect of social proof on the decisions we all make every day. We trust the opinions of others and, often, subconsciously act the way others act. Seeing someone else doing it takes away the fear. It proves, subconsciously, that it is the correct and proper way of acting. It proves the product or service is worth purchasing because it does what it promises to do. With a good product or service that truly enhances your customer's situation, let social proof do the selling for you.

69 Understand this: The top sales professional in your industry fails 70% of the time.

From afar, we can only see the sales awards, President's Club trips, congratulatory emails and corporate shout-outs, but beneath those well-deserved accolades lies a pile of rejection and failure. We see the results, but not the sweat and tears that went into the final totals. We celebrate the wins, but can't always see the trail of losses. Winning in sales includes a lot of losing, and sometimes we think those at the top are special, somehow. They don't seem to suffer the same tribulations we do, and therefore we think we are doing something wrong. We feel as though we aren't in their class, because things certainly don't go as smoothly for us. However, we must keep in mind that any sales professional who has reached the top of the mountain will undoubtedly endure many of the same pitfalls and frustrations we do. They just keep going. They persist and focus on the positive, which gives off an aura of success. That, in turn, helps attract more success. But always remember they have battled through challenges, just as we all do.

70 Give, give and give again.

There is a great little book called The Go-Giver, which teaches how giving is the quickest and most sustaining method of achieving success. Give the customer what they want. Give the company an honest effort. Give a colleague a helping hand. Give a stranger a kind word or glance. Help others achieve their goals. By giving, consistently, we do tremendous good, while amassing a tidal wave of goodwill and positivity. Helping others propels us to higher levels and feels good at the same time!

*To learn more about the people and books we've highlighted, visit: **SaleSurgeBook.com**

71 Be proud of what you do.

Can your friends, family and customers sense the pride in your product or service pouring from your very being every time you enter the room. Does everyone know what you do and how it can benefit others? This deep-rooted belief is necessary to overcome the challenges and tribulations that come with a sales career. If you don't truly believe and exude pride in your offering, you need to find a new one. You'll never achieve your best by selling something you know, deep down, isn't capable of adding tremendous value for your customer. But when you find the product that lights your fire and you *want* to offer to everyone you know - for *their* good - you'll succeed, enjoy your work and live a happy life.

72 Make the guarantee.

There are few things that can remove a buyer's trepidation like a risk-free guarantee. "Try my widget, and if you don't like it, return it for a full refund." This kind of guarantee tells your customer that they have *absolutely nothing* to lose by trying. So why, then, wouldn't they try? A guarantee also demonstrates the level of confidence you have in your product. "Try my sheets for 30 days, and if you don't love them, return them for your money back." "Take these pain-relievers for two weeks, and if you don't notice a difference, return them for a full refund." Additionally, guarantees can be attached to more than simply your product. It can also be an additional add-on to YOU. "If you join our service, I'll help get you going so you see that return on investment within a month." "I guarantee I can help you increase your bottom line." "I'll be at your office at 9am sharp to fix the issue you are having." Each of these guarantees - whether tied to a product, service or you personally - sets a tone of confidence and removes any doubt the prospective customer may have about doing business with you.

73 Get to know Dale Carnegie.

His classic, <u>How to Win Friends and Influence People</u>, has provided the foundation for countless self-help and business leaders, and is the perfect starting-point for anyone wanting to succeed in life - or sales. This is the perfect primer for sales professionals that need to get along with, and influence, other human beings. In other words, it is for all of us! A big tip from this priceless book that sticks in my mind always, thanks to Mr. Carnegie - always use a person's name. It personalizes your relationship and shows them you listen and you care! Thank you Dale Carnegie for this treasure of a book. (Sounds like a fawning Amazon review, doesn't it.)

*To learn more about the people and books we've highlighted, visit: **SaleSurgeBook.com**

74 The funnel is power.

The more qualified, potential customers you have to talk to, the more sales you are lined up to make. This fact gives you two tremendous gifts - confidence and the power to walk away. If you have five meetings scheduled with prospective customers today, you won't put additional pressure on any one of those meetings. You'll have subconscious confidence that it will be a good day, simply because you have built a prospecting framework for success. If, during your first meeting, things go south, it won't ruin your day or steal your mojo. After all, you have four more qualified prospects to call on. In fact, this underlying confidence will come out during your presentations and conversations, regardless of whether that is your intention or not. There are few things that can kill a sale as quickly as a salesperson who reeks of desperation. The salesperson who absolutely *needs* to make a sale often will not. Prospective customers can sense this desperation, which often transcends subtly into aggression. This confidence - in numbers, odds and probability - will reduce the pressure and give you the ability to walk away without a sale. Not that you *want* to walk away, just that you *can* without major repercussions. And prospects can sense this as well. This allows you to approach the conversation with the prospects well-being in mind, rather than your own. And yes, prospects can sense this as well. The key to this subconscious power is to fill your funnel with an ample supply of qualified potential customers, which will eliminate any desperation on your part and allow you to find great solutions that help the right prospects.

75 Be social.

Not necessarily the life-of-the-party kind of social. I mean social, as in social media. Connect with like-minded people - customers, colleagues, vendors, counterparts, managers, etc. You will, over time, build a network of similar professionals who you can support and learn from. In good times, you can help each other improve, through learning and sharing of best practices. In bad times, you can help each other stay connected and search for new opportunities. And when being social, you must be very careful about the online persona you are creating. Prospective employers and customers can search your social media, so always create a positive, professional image. Being social allows you to help others and, at times, rely on them for assistance. Being connected to other reputable sales professionals sends a clear message to prospective customers and employers - that you roll with the successful crowd. You don't have to be the outgoing, gregarious type, but you should make every attempt to be social.

76 Be the world's best copy-cat.

Watch what other successful sales and business professionals do - and do that! Provided they are legal and ethical, make a point of copying their actions, habits and methods of improvement. As with the numerous authors and sales leaders mentioned in this book, we can always learn and improve via the example of others. Over time, you'll naturally incorporate many of these positive, success-oriented habits into your own daily life. They will become second-nature and, as a result, you will improve incrementally. As you improve yourself by being a copy-cat, you'll improve your career trajectory as well.

77 Engage on their level.

What is most important to your customer, and how can you best serve those needs? Keep in mind that what seems most important to *you* may not even register with *them*. Your biggest value proposition - in your mind - may not even be a consideration for your customer. For example, perhaps you feel the biggest differentiator with your product is it's reliability. So you go in and pound the customer over the head - metaphorically - about how reliable and dependable your product is. However, what if this isn't something that they are concerned about? Perhaps they are only concerned with the operating power of your product. What if they are judging all products similar to yours on this one factor alone - its operating power. You waste all your time focusing on the wrong thing - the reliability - when they are considering, first and foremost, the operating power. When conducting a needs assessment, we need to first determine the true "hot buttons" for our customer (what is important to them) and deliver a presentation that meets those needs. Engage on their level, with what is important to them. You'll have happy customers that benefit from the value you provide.

78 Pull vs Push.

None of us want to become, or deal with, pushy salespeople. Rather, we prefer working with, and becoming, sales professionals who *pull* and attract our customers to us. Force a prospect to buy, and you may push them away. Pull them along, and they make their own decisions. Pulling a potential customer is simply educating and providing information to meet their needs, and allowing that information to pull them closer to what you offer. Push-selling is forcing your ideas and solutions on others, regardless of whether they are in the market or not. With a push model, you have a product and you are going to present that to your prospect, whether they like it or not. This may be a rapid way of getting a "yes," and most certainly a fast and direct method of getting a "no." Pushing involves using your force of ideas and influence. Pulling involves putting the impetus on the prospect. They choose to come closer to your idea, if it fits. Like fishing, you throw out the line, waiting for the right prospect to grab onto your specific bait. You pull them in, as *they* make their decisions and choices. Pulling may take longer, however it will create a more natural, customer-focused sales process on which to build long-term trust and relationships.

79 Today is the day.

The time to start your journey toward long-term sales success is today. The goal may be overwhelming, and seemingly unattainable, however today is the day to take the first step. How does one eat an elephant? One bite at a time. How does one reach a sales goal? One step, one sale, at a time. Your goals act as a compass, directing your activities and efforts toward what you ultimately desire. You may not be able to make those 100 sales today, but today you can build a process toward that first sale, which can be repeated 99 more times. A small step today - repeated every day this year - will be 365 small steps. In other words, a long way that you will travel, once you get started! Today! Right now. Today you learn something new to become a more complete professional. You take one of the tips in this book and incorporate it into your daily sales routine. You make a new contact, or reach out to a new prospect. Today is the day you take the first step. As you take these steps and look back, you'll be amazed at how far you've come. Today is the day to begin!

80 Be uncomfortable.

Quite often, the most uncomfortable situations are the ones with the biggest potential for gain. The more intense and painful the workout, the better the results. Only when you ask her out can she say yes. The more direct and pointed the question, the better your customer's answer will be at creating clarity around their needs and your solution. In sales, the condition of being uncomfortable is often the road to higher achievement. For example, perhaps you may fear public speaking and prefer interacting with prospects via phone and email. However, one day you receive an offer to speak to 100 captive prospects in an auditorium. While uncomfortable to you, this opportunity will allow you to leverage your time and personally reach a large group of potential customers. Will you accept the uncomfortable, allowing you to grow your reach, influence and business? Or will you shrink back behind the keyboard and turn your back on rapid growth and success. Choosing to be uncomfortable occasionally will unlock areas for personal growth, allow you to improve and help you reach higher levels of sales success.

81 Incremental steps to victory.

As I asked in Tip #79, how do you eat an elephant? One bite at a time. How do you create a successful sales career? One day - one sale - at a time. On his wonderful podcast, Brian Buffini says, "we often overestimate how much we can accomplish in a year, but we underestimate how much we can accomplish in a decade." A career cannot be built in a week or a year, but it can become hugely successful over the course of years or decades. In sales, as in many other career paths, the arch of our career often becomes easier the longer we persevere. One step today - repeated over and over - is the way to success. Like wealth, wise decisions repeated every day lead to massive results. We cannot sell enough today to reach the pinnacle and leave a legacy. However, if we do the right things today, and tomorrow, and the day after that, we will ultimately sit on top of the mountain of success.

*To learn more about the people and books we've highlighted, visit: **SaleSurgeBook.com**

82 Be objective regarding market trends.

Be honest with yourself, both before accepting a position and while working in your current endeavor. Don't get swept up by promises and hype. Is your company a top player, poised for growth? Does your product have a long-term future? Will it be phased out by another product or solution that is better-priced or more effective? When considering these, and other, factors, don't paint an overly-rosy picture. Be honest and determine, for your own good, where your product, company and leadership may be in five or ten years. If you cannot honestly see this as somewhere with long-term upside, it may be time to search elsewhere. If your product is actually a dog when compared to the rest of the field, this may not be a great place to be. Only when being honest with yourself regarding the market, and how your current company fits it, can you determine any true upside you may, or may not, have.

83 Customers lie.

Sometimes they tell you they will buy, and they don't. They tell you to stop by, and there aren't there. They tell you they aren't talking to your competition, when they are. They tell you price is the main factor, when it isn't. They tell you they like you, when they don't. They tell you your product is great, when they don't actually think so. It is our job as professionals to get to the root causes and the real truth. Because when they lie, they often don't mean to. Think about yourself for a moment, as a consumer. Think about the last time you were making a major purchase. We all lie, because in the moment we really think we *will* buy. Then something changes. We think we *won't* talk to the competition, but somehow they build a relationship with us. We think the product *is* great, until a better option appears. The point is, as a professional, it is our job to ask the right questions to sort out the truth from the lies. Because at some point, every customer - including you - lies.

84 Transactional vs. Relational Sales.

Which one best fits your sales model? A transactional sale is a one-and-done situation. You show up, make the sale and then have very little connection with the customer after that initial interaction. For example, a door to door sale of candy, baked goods or a coupon book would be a one-time, transactional sale. A relational sale, however, is a longer-term process which may include multiple transactions over time. In this model, there is an importance to your interpersonal relationship and connection. One example of a relational sale would be a pharmaceutical sales professional who routinely shows up to educate a doctor about the uses and effects of a new medication. In this example, the relationship, built on mutual needs, trust and respect, leads to, perhaps, many sales over time. It is crucial to understand which of these two sales models best fits your industry, product or service, so you can best tailor your approach. In addition, most sales professionals greatly prefer one or the other, and feel most comfortable while working within their preferred sales model.

The good news is that it is pretty much common sense, so you'll usually know and understand the best approach for any given product or service.

85 Networking for the new age.

In the past, networking to build, grow or launch a career consisted of happy-hour gatherings, swapping business cards and exchanging hand-written letters. These days - while those methods of hobnobbing may still work - professionals "network" in a host of new ways. Social media is the predominant method, allowing constant interaction and expansion of your network. You can literally connect with hiring managers, recruiters, influencers and colleagues - all while munching cheese puffs on the couch in your boxer shorts. (not that I've ever done that, of course) In other words, it is just plain easier to network and build connections than it has ever been in human history. The depth of those connections is another topic altogether, however creating for yourself a web of like-minded professionals has never been easier. Use the web and the socials to our advantage, and save yourself the trip to another boring happy hour.

86 Identify negativity and run!

In sales, we have to work with, and for, a wide variety of people. Some will share our values, beliefs, style or personality, and others will not. However, our job as professionals is to work successfully with as many people as possible. In other words, we need to play nice in the sandbox, no matter what that other kid does. There is, however, one trait that should make us turn and run, taking not a second to look back. That trait is negativity. Since so much of sales revolves around dealing with failure, we must always maintain a positive outlook and optimistic attitude. These are crucial to long-term success. When we encounter a negative person, whether a customer, colleague, manager or prospect, we must be disciplined enough to spot the behavior and remove ourselves from its influence. If a prospect is snarky and demeaning, leave. If a colleague or manager is always looking at the glass half empty, limit your time in their presence. You may not believe it, but even some established, productive customers of yours may need to be "fired" for their negativity if they drain your time and your positive emotions. Like crabs in a box, negative Nellies will drag down anyone who tries to escape the pessimistic confines. Negative people bring others down to their level. If you spend too much time around negative influences, before long you'll find yourself slipping to their level. Over time, this can have an extremely negative, and often undetected, impact on your sales results and career progression.

87 Have a goal for each call.

Before walking in the door or picking up the phone, we must always know what we aim to accomplish. After all, if you aim at nothing, you'll hit it every time. We need to be crystal clear about what "victory" looks like. Is it scheduling a meeting? Is it securing a signature for a sale? Is it finding out the name of the key decision maker? This doesn't mean you have to write it down or create a detailed spreadsheet. But at the very least, you must *know*. Without a well-defined objective, our sales calls and presentations can seem to go well, while meandering into areas that don't serve our best needs, or the customer's. Our goals for the call keep us focused and directed on well-defined objectives, which continue our sales process toward a fruitful end.

88 Relationships equal trust.

Sometimes it is difficult to trust someone you've known for a long time. And with some people, it is specifically *because* you've known them so well. However, it is nearly impossible to trust someone whom you've just met. We may get a good feeling, or establish a connection - which are both important - but it is doubtful that you can truly trust someone after just meeting him. Trust is built, gained and earned over time. Trust forms much like the foundation of a home - one brick at a time. One interaction at a time. And once this foundation of trust is laid, it allows you to overcome many other flying obstacles. Like a house with a strong foundation in a storm, it's strength will protect the home and allow it to continue standing after the raindrops have dissipated. Invest the time to lay each brick, day after day.

89 Get the meeting.

It is extremely difficult to sell anything without a captive audience who will listen to your story. Sure, direct mail, TV commercials, radio ads and the like can work, but even they rely on a direct audience engaging with their content. The same is true for sales professionals who get up and pound the pavement each day. We need to meet with a potential customer before we can expect them to purchase from us. Depending on the sale, the meeting may be 30 seconds. Or in some more complex sales, it may be just one in a long series of multi-person, multi-layered meetings. Step one, though, is to get that first meeting. From there you may work toward an eventual sale, or you may face head-on, smack-to-the-face rejection. But nothing happens without that first meeting.

90 Ask for the referral now.

The best time to ask for a referral is immediately after a customer buys from you. At that moment, they are both intellectually and emotionally tied to their purchase. They feel it is the best decision for them, otherwise they would not have purchased. So this moment where their satisfaction and happiness regarding our product is the highest is the optimal time to ask who else you could delight. The strange thing is that directly after the sale is often the time we, as sales professionals, would rather *NOT* ask for the referral. Things have gone so well that the customer has made a purchase from us, and the temptation is for us to not want to screw it up! We don't want to keep asking for things when we just got the main thing we wanted in the first place. But the truth is that for long term professional growth and success, we need an overflowing pipeline of potential customers. A sale today can help us meet our quota this quarter, but those two referrals might help get us over the finishing line next quarter, and the quarter after that. The best time to start building that momentum, by asking for the referral, is now!

91 Uncover the hot button.

At the root of every purchase we make is a need, or hot button. This is the motivator, which gives us a kick in the rear and forces us to act. For example, when I get tired of walking everywhere, this hot button of sore legs and long commute times will become my hot button for buying a car. If my dog only listens to my commands when I reward him with sweet cookie treats, the hot button of always cleaning up after him causes me to shop for treats. It is not just that I *want* to buy something, but rather it is a specific hot button, or pain point, that puts me into buying action. This pain I need to dull is much more of a motivator than simply a potential need I may have. The pain, or hot button, gets me off the couch and into motion to make a purchase. As sales professionals, we need to find this specific hot button and make the connection, positioning our product or service as the solution. (only if it is, of course) If you walk onto my car lot, I can certainly try to sell you a car. After all, why else would you be there? But what if I can find out that you recently had a new baby girl and have a deep need for security, in the form of a large, safe SUV, to transport her around. By deciphering and tapping into this need, I can immediately introduce you to our biggest and safest SUV, thus solving the problem caused by your hot button. It is a much more efficient way to sell, as well as a much better experience for the customer! The problem is that we, as consumers, don't walk around with our hot buttons typed on our forehead. It is up to professional sales professionals to help us verbalize these pain points, in order to meet our most deeply-felt needs. By uncovering the hot button, you help both your customer and yourself.

92 Price must come last.

The reason is because it is *relative*. What do I
mean? Let's give you an example. I want to sell
you my product for $1000. It is the best product
and everyone loves it. Do you want to buy it?
Chances are you just said "No!" The reason is
because you don't even know what the product
is or does, and there is absolutely no value that
can be added to your life if you purchase my
product. But how about I lay it out this way. "I
know you have been struggling with doing the
laundry for your large family. You have a
spouse and four kids, and every week you are
spending $50 using the local laundromat to
wash your clothes. Not to mention the time and
travel expenses of getting you to and from the
laundromat. So is it right to estimate you are
spending about 10-15 hours per month and
about $200 per month doing your family's
laundry? Wow, what a hassle! How about I
show you my brand new, top-of-the-line
washing machine. You can stay right at home
and not have to travel across town to the
laundromat. This will give you those 10-15
hours back, to do all those things you've been

needing or wanting to do. You can spend so much more time with your kids, or you can get so many other chores done around the house. Imagine that enjoyment and freedom! Also, did we estimate you are currently spending about $200 a month doing laundry at the laundromat? So you're spending about $2400 a year! We can also save you a lot of money by doing your laundry at home. You can have this top of the line, brand new washing machine in your home for just $1000. That's what you are already spending in less than half a year, with all the hassle of doing laundry at the laundromat! Would that extra $1400 a year be useful? This sounds like a great fit for you and your family. Would you like to buy my product for $1000?" As we can see, only once I established the value of my product does the price enter into the equation. It is always relative to the value it brings to your customer's life, which is why we want to establish that value first, so we can juxtapose it against the price of our product or service.

93 Shut up and listen.

How often do you find yourself in a conversation with a customer or prospect, and while they are talking you are already thinking about the next thing you are going to say? While they are expressing something to you, you are thinking of the perfect comeback to counter their point and get the sale. We all do it, and we all need to stop. What we should do instead is practice "active listening." By listening actively, we completely and totally focus on what they are saying, without thinking ahead to our comeback. If we really listen, the conversation will be more natural and, most importantly, we'll uncover the truly beneficial information to help both the customer and ourselves. Customers usually don't care how much we know, evidenced by how much we spew about our product and service. They do want to know how much we *care* - about their situation, their life and their problems. Shut up and listen, and they will intuitively feel that we are on their side, looking for the perfect solution.

94 Most prospects are not a fit.

We need to view "prospects" in a detached, objective way, until we establish a relationship and form a basis to move forward in our sales process. The reason is as much for our own sanity regarding the basic fact that most prospects are not a fit. In other words, they won't buy from us. Either they don't need what we have to offer, or they don't need it *now*. If we approach our day-to-day prospecting duties with this overarching mindset, we can continue to "fill the funnel" with prospects, while never getting too attached to any one of them. If we know most of them are not a fit, we can more-easily filter through the 90% that we know won't buy from us to find the 10% that will. That way, each "failure" is nothing more than a step in the planned process. We know we'll fail a whole lot in order to succeed, because we know most prospects are not a fit. Our mindset should expect success unquestionably, but only after sifting through the dirt to reach the gold.

95 Just leave me some information.

When you stop in on a cold call and this is the response, what the person is actually saying is, "I don't need what you have, and I really don't even know you or like you, so why would I buy something from you anyway? Besides, I'm busy and never asked you to stop here to see me in the first place." And you can bet that within ten minutes of you leaving...actually, make that two minutes...your materials that they asked you to leave will be comfortably nestled in the nearest garbage receptacle. You leave materials and very quickly they end up in the trash. Think Forky from Toy Story 4. At the first opportunity, he was in a garbage can. The same holds true for the materials you leave when they say, "Just leave me some information."

96 Information is key.

Grab it during every visit. What is the customer's spouse's name? In what town does he live? What are his hobbies? His kids names? Their schools? You never know when this information will come in handy - not only for proving that you care and listen, but also because it is just the right way to treat people. When we care about the details of their life, they can FEEL that we care. This is how trustful relationships are built, whether in dating scenarios, friendships or business associations. Gather the information when you can and use it when appropriate to show you view your customer as a real person, rather than as a sale.

97 It's not about the watch.

Many years ago, while home for the summer
during my college years, I attended a pretty
raucous party in my hometown. While escaping
the hot, summer sun and chatting with some
friends inside the house, I was introduced to
one of my buddies' college pals. Nice guy,
albeit a little full of himself. As we all stood
around talking and sipping cold ones, this
friend launched into his life story, focusing
mostly on his sales career. He was a veteran,
you see, well-versed and immersed in the ways
of the world. I don't even recall what he said he
was selling, but you could tell he was trying to
be right out of Wolf of Wall Street. (a movie
not released until decades later) He sure was a
mover and a shaker, at least hearing his version
of his fast-paced life making deals and cashing
checks. The best part of his story was when he
gave us what he called "the biggest key to
making a lot of money in sales." He said that
key, the holy grail for sales success as far as he
was concerned, was that you had to wear a
large, gaudy, expensive watch. He said by
wearing that watch, prospects knew he was a

successful, wealthy and confident professional from whom they should buy whatever it was he was selling. That's it! I could have saved you the other 99 tips for sales success and wrote a short, impactful book about buying the expensive watch. You probably have guessed by now, however, that in the decades since I've learned that a watch doesn't make you a successful, wealthy and confident professional from whom your customers should buy whatever it is you are selling. The other 99 tips in this book lay out the foundation, and I don't think having a watch is mentioned. Yes, you want to dress in a clean, professional and appropriate manner for your industry. And yes, some customers may be impressed with your expensive-looking clothes or accessories. But you never want to shift focus away from your message and onto your clothes - watch, tie, hat, shirt, car....whatever. And it is also true that you will push some prospects away if you "look" like you are trying too hard to impress them with stuff. The message I get from a salesman who overdoes the showy stuff if that he is trying to make up for what he lacks in substance and value his products can deliver for me. I'm buying the value he brings me, not the watch on his wrist. I don't know what that fellow is up to nowadays, but I do know that, decades later, not one person has ever bought from me because of my watch. But it does help me get to the appointment on time!

98 Call on the decision-maker.

In some organizations or companies, only one person has the power to say "yes" to a purchase or buying decision. In others, team members at varying levels may have the authorization to buy what you are selling. In either case, you want to make sure to make your full presentation to the person who is able to buy. It sounds simple, but just finding out this information (see rule # 96) may save you a great amount of time and frustration. There are few things worse for the salesperson than giving a rock-solid, captivating presentation, only to find out that the person on the other end cannot make the decision even if it were the best product in the history of products. In some sales models, you will easily know who can and cannot buy. In other industries, you may have to clarify, or flat-out ask, before scheduling and delivering the presentation. Save time and energy and present your product or service to the right person - the person who can buy!

99 Plan your travel wisely.

It is not necessarily how *much* you work that counts, but rather how much you work *smartly* that matter most. Rather than driving haphazardly all over creation to see all of your clients, customers and prospects, you'd be much better served to take time to plan your route. Plan the entire day, from the first stop to the last. As Abraham Lincoln said, "Give me six hours to chop down a tree and I will spend the first four sharpening the ax." In many cases, you'll find that this extra time planning will allow you to be much more efficient and complete the planned visits in much less time than it would have had you simply went out with no real agenda in mind. And when you finish these visits early, don't feel guilty or lazy, because you'll be able to fit in more business-related activities to supercharge your sales and grow your income.

100 The hottest days are the best.

Years ago, my dear friend and high school baseball coach gave me some wonderful words of wisdom, which have helped me tackle adversity and reach for higher goals throughout my life. It was swelteringly hot and humid as we warmed up before that afternoon's ballgame. The kind of day where you drip sticky sweat after just minutes outside. As we stretched prior to the ballgame, many of my teammates, probably including myself, complained about the uncomfortable heat and humidity. We were really not happy playing in this kind of thick heat. "You know fellas," our coach said with a calming, quiet demeanor, "This is the perfect day to play a ballgame, and a big advantage for us." I didn't understand what he meant. After all, we were dripping with sweat and completely uncomfortable, and the game hadn't even begun! How could this be a perfect day to play? "Think about it guys. Right now our opponent over there is doing the same thing we are - complaining about the heat. They are saying the same things we are. But I always try to flip it around for myself. I always tell myself that these days are the *BEST* days to play. When the conditions are lousy, when I don't feel great, when there is a difficult obstacle in my way, such as this 100 degree temperature - that is *EXACTLY* when I *WANT* to play, because I know I have an advantage." He was starting to get through to us. "If I know the other team is complaining and feeling like the weather, or whatever, is working against them, I use that to my advantage! They are right, because this day will work against them and *for* me! This is the perfect day to play, because I automatically start out with a mental advantage!" No surprise, we went out that day and won. And for the rest of my career, those hot, humid, uncomfortable days were the days I looked forward to playing the most. We can translate that mindset to our sales career. When things are difficult, when it rains, when it is hot, when we are behind our quota, when customers slam the door in our face, when our manager micromanages, when customers complain, when clients make unreasonable demands - these are the BEST days to sell. These are the BEST days to succeed, win and grow our career. Because these are the days that force our competitors to wilt. These days cause others to tuck their tail and go back to bed. But we persevere and embrace these days. We look forward to them, and we enjoy these days. Because these are the best days to sell, to succeed and to win!

Our bonus for you...

For the full list of links we mentioned in the book visit SaleSurgeBook.com

If you enjoyed Sales Surge Sequel, you may also like the first book.....

Sales Surge: 50 Secrets to Propel Your Sales Career With Less Stress and More Fun!

Available on Amazon and Audible!

We hope these tips will help you supercharge your sales career, so you enjoy the sales surge you are looking for.

Thanks for reading!